First World War
and Army of Occupation
War Diary
France, Belgium and Germany

4 DIVISION
11 Infantry Brigade,
Brigade Trench Mortar Battery
1 August 1916 - 31 August 1916

WO95/1500/2

Published by

The Naval & Military Press Ltd

Unit 10 Ridgewood Industrial Park,

Uckfield, East Sussex,

TN22 5QE England

Tel: +44 (0) 1825 749494

www.naval-military-press.com

www.nmarchive.com

This diary has been reprinted in facsimile from the original. Any imperfections are inevitably reproduced and the quality may fall short of modern type and cartographic standards.

© **Crown Copyright**
Images reproduced by permission of The National Archives, London, England, 2015.

Contents

Document type	Place/Title	Date From	Date To
Heading	WO95/1500/2		
Heading	4th Division. IIth Trench Mortar Battery. June 30th To August. 31st. 1915		
Miscellaneous	A Form. Messages And Signals.		
War Diary	Maillet Mailley	01/08/1916	01/08/1916
War Diary	Ypres	27/08/1916	31/08/1916
Heading	Trench Mortar Battery. Nov. 1916		

WO 95/1500/(2)

4th DIVISION.

11th TRENCH MORTAR BATTERY.

JUNE 30th to AUGUST 31st.

1916.

"A" Form.
MESSAGES AND SIGNALS.

Army Form C. 2121.

Prefix .... Code .... m.	Words	Charge	This message is on a/c of:	Recd .... m.
Office of Origin and Service Instructions.	Sent			Date ....
	At .... m.		.... Service.	From ....
	To		(Signature of "Franking Officer.")	By ....
	By			

TO { D.A.G. Ban

Sender's Number.	Day of Month.	In reply to Number.	
* T.M. 0/103	30/8/1916	—	A A A

Herewith "War Diary" for period June 30th — August 31st/16
I cannot give you any previous information, as the
Battery was not in my Command before this date,
no previous records can be found. aaa

From O.T. 11th T.M. Bty.
Place
Time

The above may be forwarded as now corrected.   (Z)   S.T. Read Lt.

Censor.   Signature of Addressee or person authorised to telegraph in his name.

* This line should be erased if not required.

WAR DIARY
or
INTELLIGENCE SUMMARY
(Erase heading not required.)

Army Form C. 2118.

June 30th to July 27th/16

T.M. 7/I

VOC 1-2-3

Place	Date	Hour	Summary of Events and Information	Remarks and references to Appendices
	June 30th/16 5pm		The June 30th/16 the 111th Brigade took up position prior to the attack S.W. of BEAUMONT - HAMEL	
	July 1st 6.30am		The attack of the 111th T.M. B'ty's were to have then supported places	
MAILLET MAILLEY	1.8.16	7.30	The Zero Hr arrived zero timer for 7.30am. At 7.20am the Battery had in gun Emplacen- began the attack not going own into action in No mans Land. Several rounds off for the Enemy trenches & then their stokes Mortars each gun fired into action 150 Bombs. Of the 10Rts it was impossible to get him communication up to them. Those that advanced to the Enemy wire were Knocked out. But then tried there No 16 no 18 Stay Combat att Clark Leay Pave gave in the Enemy's Trench after destroying their wire. Although the Enemy try to meet to escape out & Enemy on their Continuous Bomb. The Brigade also well gave their Machine. The Bomb Brigade. The total loss of the MAILLEY MAILLET + Canal dy junta on attack of 26 Machs 1 Officer + 25 other ranks out of a total of 5 officers + 72 other ranks. Later the Brigade moved to YPRES	
2/PRE.	2.0.			

O.C.
111th T.M. B'ty

WAR DIARY or INTELLIGENCE SUMMARY

Army Form C. 2118.

July 27th to August 31st/16 T.M. 7/11

Place	Date	Hour	Summary of Events and Information	Remarks and references to Appendices
YPRES.	27th/8/16		On the night of the 27th/28th July/16 the Front was taken over in the PILCKEM Sector from the 3rd Guards Brigade, the units relieved in the Sector on the night of the 12th/13th August/16 by the 10th Infantry Brigade, & proceeded into Rest Camp on the ELVERDINGHE – POPERINGHE Road, 1 mile from POPERINGHE.	
"	12-13th/8/16		During the time we were in the whole Front was generally quiet. With the exception of the night of the 9th/10th August.	
"		11 P.M.	On that night there was an intense artillery & trench mortars bombardment on the part of the enemy. Which lasted from 11pm. Until 12.30 am.	
"		11.45	About 11.45 p.m. the enemy sent over gas, in two waves, at an interval of about 5 minutes. Our artillery opened fire shortly after the enemy started the bombardment, about 7 minutes after the gas two silhouettes, we opened our artillery in "Barrage", no mans land.	
"	21st/8/16		On the night of the 21st/22nd August /16 we relieved the 7th Canadian Infantry Brigade in the HOOGE Sector. The whole Front was quiet on the 22nd, 23rd, 24th & 25th of August.	
"			On the morning of the 26th August /16, about 9.30 am the enemy opened an artillery & trench mortar bombardment on the whole Front Sector, about 10 a.m. which lasted until 10.30 a.m. The casualties amongst the infantry were light, we had no casualties. Station.	O.C. 1/15 T.M. Bty
"	21st-27/8/16		We joined in retaliation with our artillery. From observation a good deal of damage was done to the Enemy Trenches, the Front support trench (KENNEDY) who rather heavily damaged. Otherwise no further appreciable damage has been	O.C. 1/15 T.M. Bty

WAR DIARY
or
INTELLIGENCE SUMMARY

Army Form C. 2118.

July 27th – August 31st/16
Colonel:— T.M. 7/11

Place	Date	Hour	Summary of Events and Information	Remarks and references to Appendices
23rd–31st/8/16			Coy to N.Rlk Gds. all toms guns, & club Inst. Cadet for any action on Dir. Parts: draft round guns	

4th DIVISION.

TRENCH MORTAR BATTERY.

NOVEMBER 1916.

www.ingramcontent.com/pod-product-compliance
Lightning Source LLC
Chambersburg PA
CBHW051529190426
43193CB00045BA/2673